A Catalog for the
Fred Martin Exhibition
at the Art Foundry Gallery
April 7-30, 2011

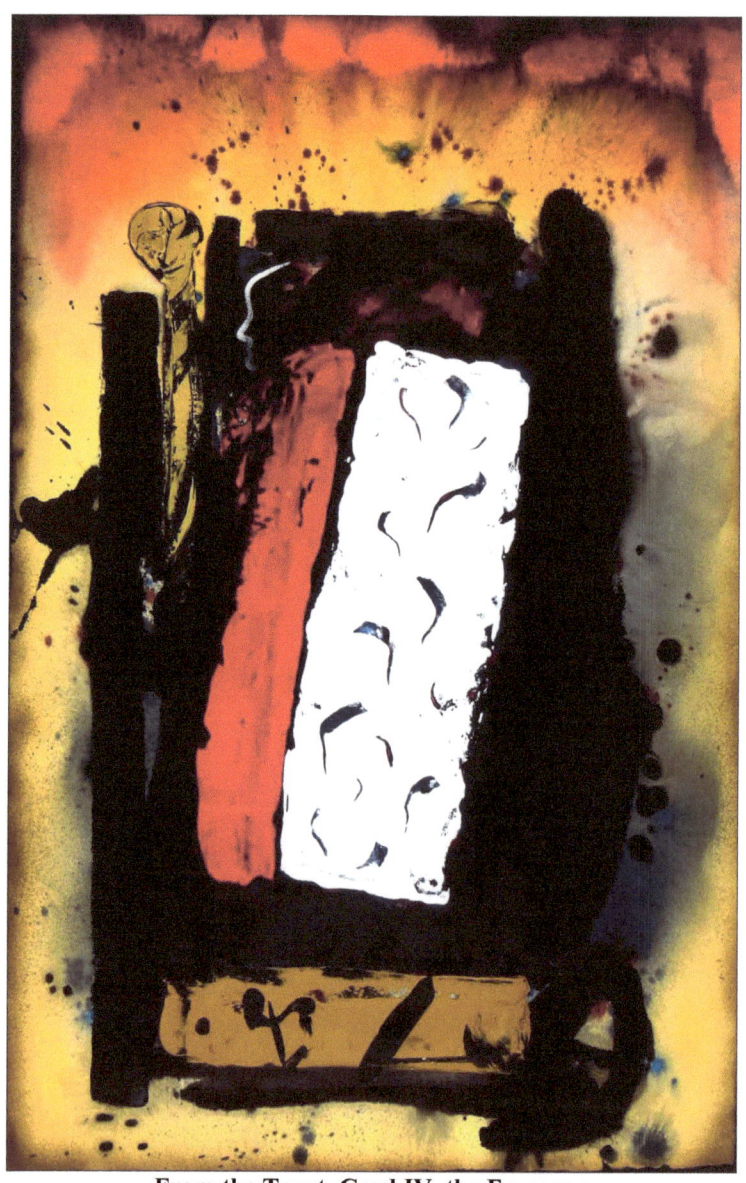

From the Tarot, Card IV, the Emperor
January 2, 1995. Acrylic on paper, 68 x 44 inches.

A Catalog for the
Fred Martin Exhibition
at the Art Foundry Gallery
April 7-30, 2011

Note that although all of this
work is available at the gallery
during the exhibition,
there is not enough space to show
all of it at one time.
Please enquire at the desk
to see a piece that may not
be on exhibition
at the time you are here.

Green Gates Press
2011

A Catalog for
Fred Martin Exhibition at the Art Foundry Gallery
April 7-30, 2011

For my wife,
Stephanie Dudek

Green Gates Press
Copyright 2011

ISBN 978-1-257-11841-0

Introduction

A studio note from March 1995 when the 1995 work in this show was being made, and which applies also to the 2011 work in the show—

Why is much of this work "after" the Tarot?
As Bach's *Well Tempered Clavier* gave him an objective structure through which to pour the flow of musical life, so I can use the Major Arcana images of the Tarot as shapes through which to pour the adventure of painting...

To paint is to see and make and remember all of the painting and living I have done; it is to shape and see the painting and living I will do. "Art as Spiritual work"—the words degrade, the act exalts. Don't say "Painting as..." just do it.

Painting and living: they are the same:

Some Background about the Tarot...

The earliest known deck was made in the mid 15th Century by an unknown artist for a prominent member of the Visconti-Sforza family, then rulers of Milan. Whatever was before that deck is unknown, but that deck includes the first images of what has come to be the Tarot as we know it today—the 22 picture cards (today's Major Arcana), plus the four suits of Staves, Cups, Swords, Coins (today's Minor Arcana).[1]

Most likely in the beginning the cards were used for what is now the gambling game *Tarocchi,*[2] but people then and now were superstitious... and the fall of cards in a game of chance might easily reflect the fall of fate in the game of life. Thus, fortune tellers would study the cards, particularly the picture cards of the Major Arcana for what

---

[1] Today's playing cards use clubs, hearts, spades and diamonds for the original stave, cup, sword and coin.
[2] Hence the later, French name *Tarot*

they might suggest to say to the gullible about their past and troubles, their future and joys.

So the Tarocchi/Tarot deck continued from the 15th to the end of the 18th Century. Along the way, the original design of the cards was changed so that when *Tarocchi* is played now there is no right side up or upside down because those positions in dealing Tarot for fortune telling had come to mean good luck (up) and or bad luck (down).[3]

All of that began to change at the end of the 18th Century with Etteila's claiming an ancient Egyptian origin to the cards. The reasoning was that Egyptian hieroglyphics are of ancient and obscure meaning—therefore surely magical—and the images of the Tarot are of ancient and obscure meaning and so must also be Egyptian and magical. Thus, as the 19th Century came and went, the occult obscure of any handy tradition was brought into a most illicit coupling with any other available occult obscure, was somehow associated to and mixed with the imagery of the Tarot, and the magic and mystery of the Tarot for divination grew and grew. To the rational mind, the Tarot is more than 200 years of quacks and charlatans scavenging abracadabra from the garbage of history to impress the gullible of today.

But, as modern psychology has demonstrated in the work of Jung and others, there are in the depths of the individual psyche images as alive (though in different clothes) as they were in the caves of Lascaux or the walls of Pompeii, in the cathedrals of Europe or the temples of India. These beings and situations—archetypes, Jung called them—show up in even so humble a place as the Tarot... and that is why the Major Arcana, a mere 22 playing cards with pictures on them, has lasted for centuries and remains today a place of mystery and power for those who know how to open its images.

---

[3] See examples from a late 19th Century *Tarocchi* deck at top of previous page.

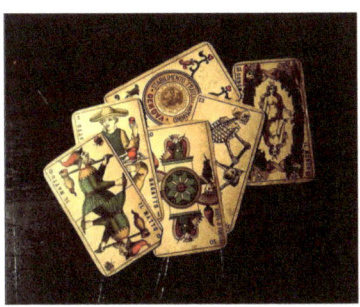

A selection of cards from the late 19th Century
Piedmont Tarocchi Deck that started it all.

My own experience of the Tarot began in 1950 with the Tarocchi deck my first wife had inherited from her great uncle who had brought it when he emigrated from Italy to the San Joaquin Valley at the end of the 19th Century. I thought the images were curious and so made out of cardboard a three foot high "Trajan's Column" coiled with the Major Arcana images drawn in the style of 17th Century German alchemical engravings.

The column lasted maybe six months and I did not think about the Tarot again until the late 1970's early 80's when bored with what I had been making, I decided I wanted an external "objective" source of images—something "archetypal"—and remembered the old cards in the closet. I began with a series of drawings of the Major Arcana, then made my own linoblock images for each card and printed hundreds of combinations of them, and then made a portfolio of etchings —*The Tarot of California*—with 3EP Press in Palo Alto in 1982.

After that, life took different paths until finally, as in the early 1995 studio note quoted above, once again I wanted something outside my own subjectivity to provide impulse and structure for my work. The large acrylics on paper in this exhibition are the result.

I made the paintings in the spring of 1995, and when the opportunity came for an exhibition at the College of Fine

Arts of Shanghai University that fall—what else to show but these? Realizing that the Chinese audience would need some background in order to understand the image sources, I made a catalog with a brief history of the Tarot and an explanation of how these particular images of mine had come to be...

"...not representing the images in an identifiable way, but entering instead the feeling of the image as I have come to know it, and out of that feeling (as a composer makes a melody of his feeling from a poem) painting until an image of my feeling appeared in the paint upon the paper.

"It may help you in looking at the paintings, however, to have a brief written outline of my own adaptation of the traditional meanings assigned to each of the cards I have painted—the words, so to speak, of the painted music you see. Remember, though, that what follows are only the words. Hardly a trace of the originating Tarot images remain in the paintings themselves."

The Shanghai catalog then gave a sentence or two for each painting in the show. I have provided those sentences with the correspondent images of the paintings in the following pages.

The Shanghai catalog ended with "Do not look for these Tarot images in the paintings; the words of the images only start the musical search that is the act of painting itself."

So, here again so many years later, although I have again provided the words, don't look for their images in the paintings. Words are words, a painting is a painting. Look at it and see what you see for yourself

(Please note that all of the paintings from the 1995 group are acrylic on paper, 68 x 44 inches.)

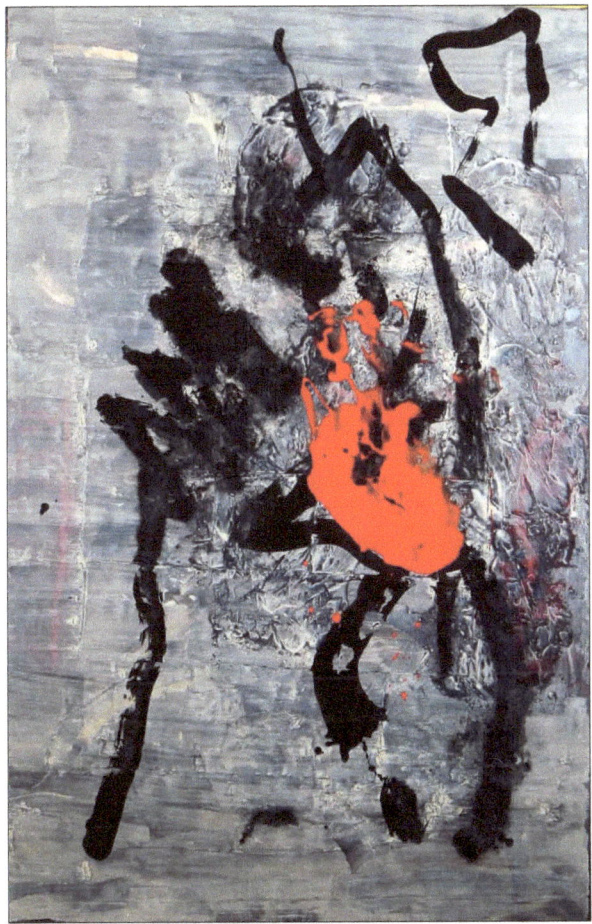

The Fool.
(marked October 95 and with the words "Crazy Dance")

From the 1995 Shanghai Catalog—
This card is for you. The Fool is traditionally the unnumbered card of the Major Arcana. He is you as you wander into the wilderness, homeless and dressed in mismatched clothes. A dog barks and bites your leg to hurry you out of town.

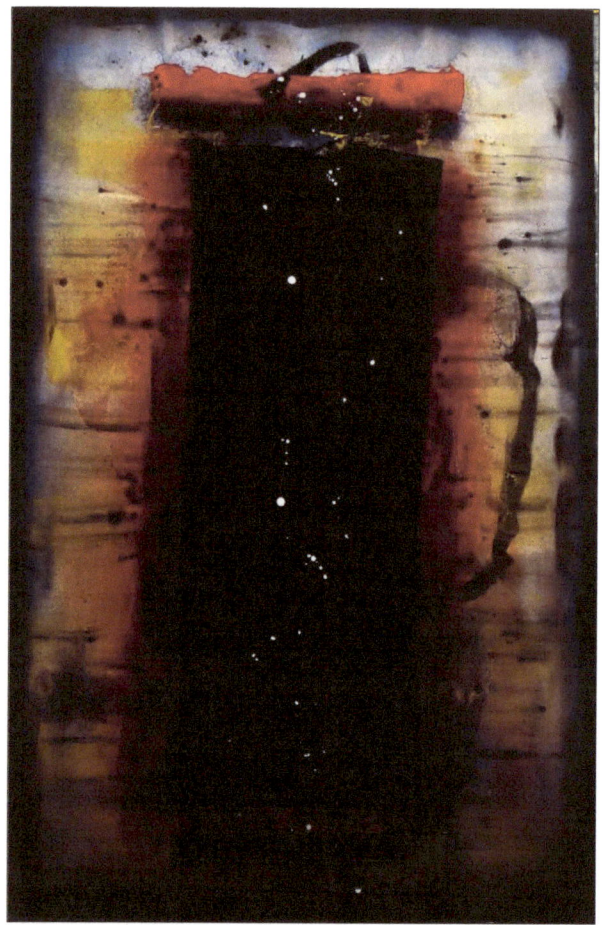

Tarot II. The High Priestess.
(dated 2/15/95)

From the 1995 Shanghai Catalog—
The High Priestess is the ruler woman of sacred things.
She goes by the book, by the word and by your own blood
traced above her body of starry night.

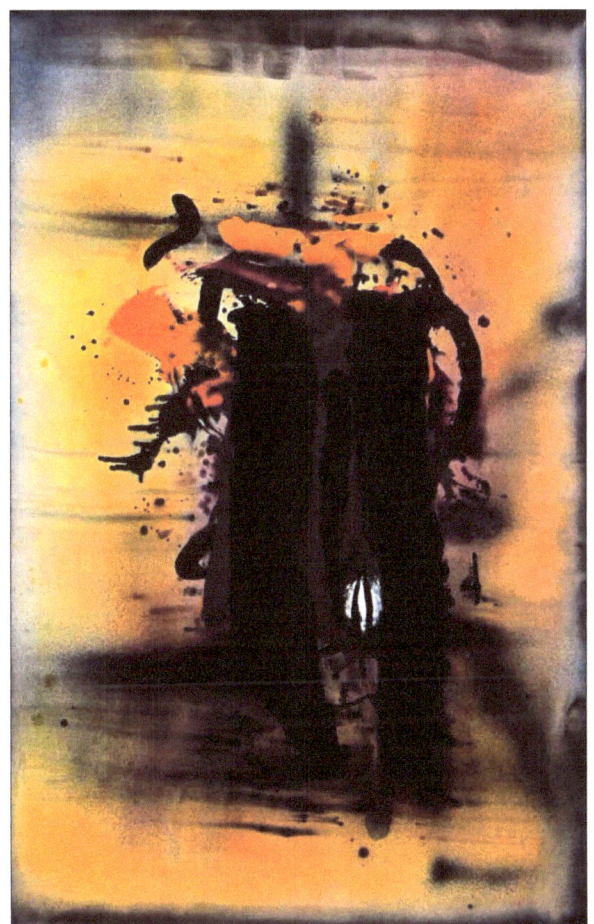

Tarot III. The Empress.
(dated 2/12/95)

From the 1995 Shanghai Catalog—
The Empress is the ruler woman of this world where all things obey her whim and fear her wrath.

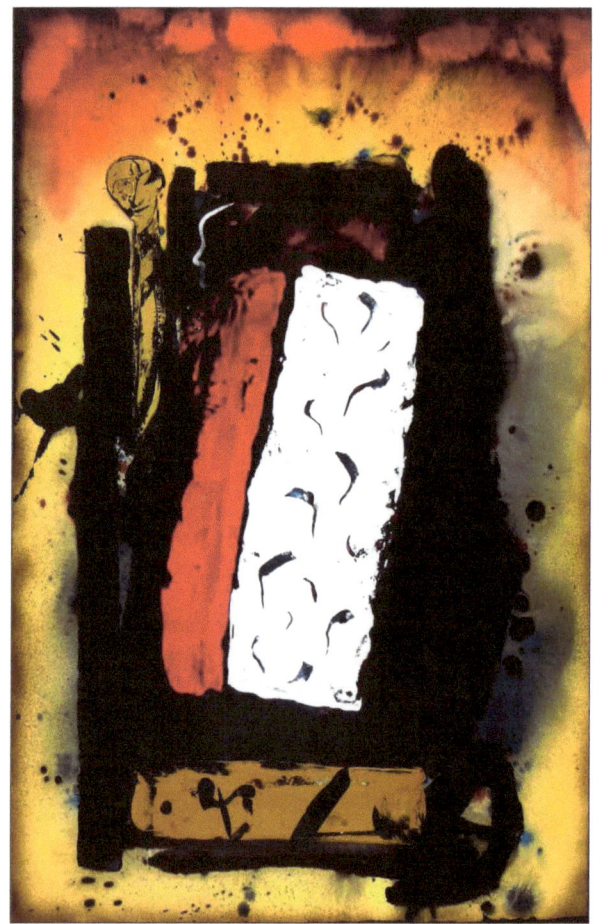

Tarot IV. The Emperor
(dated 1/2/95)

From the 1995 Shanghai Catalog—
The Emperor is the ruler man of a world of force, deception and conquest.

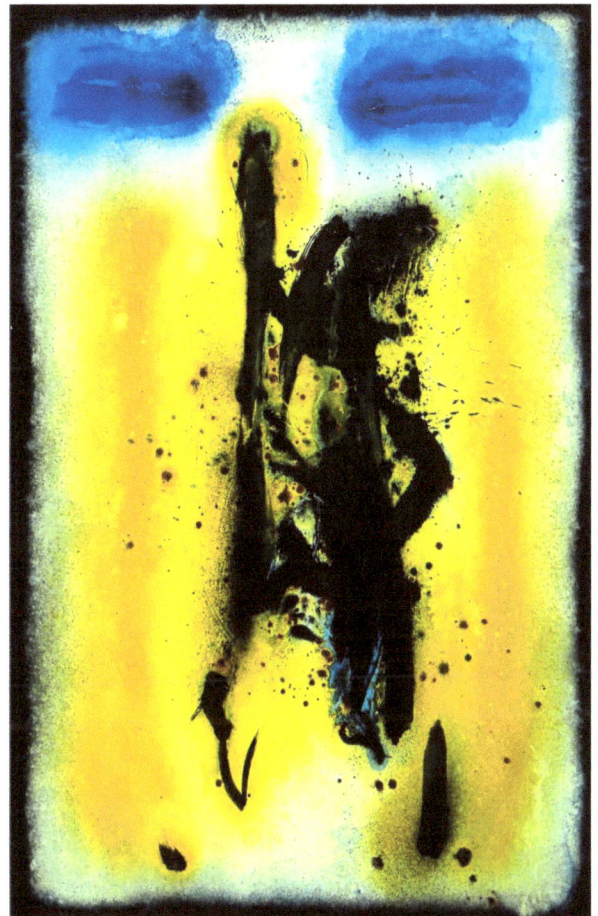

Tarot V. The High Priest
(dated 2/19/95)

From the 1995 Shanghai Catalog—
The High Priest is the ruler man of the world of spirit like the Emperor rules the world of matter. The High Priest guides you by the shepherd's rod that guides the sheep.

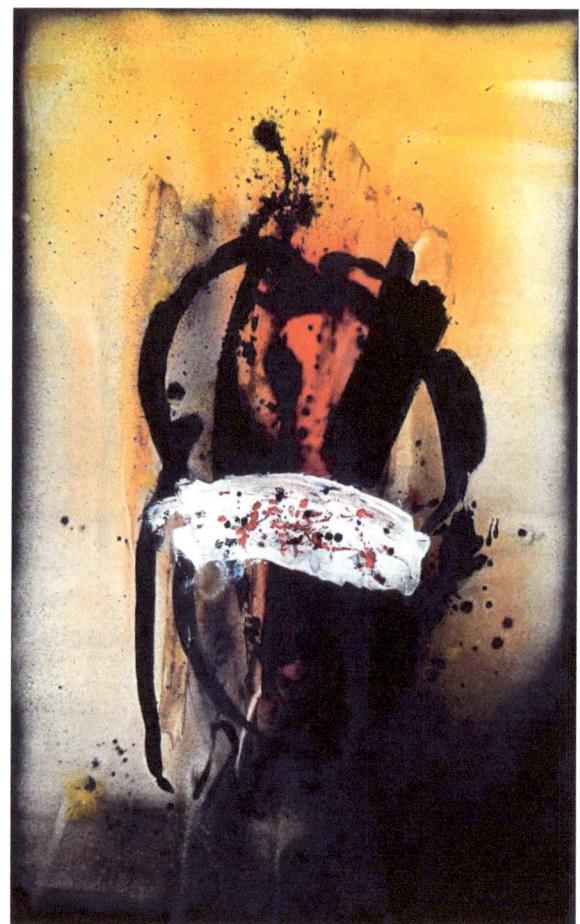

Tarot VI. The Lovers
(dated 1/19/95)

From the 1995 Shanghai Catalog—
In the cards it's the problem of choice between marrying for money or marrying for love; for you it's a promise in blood beyond rich and poor, sickness and health, all the way to the heartbreak of death.

Tarot VIII. Justice
(dated 3/16/95)

From the 1995 Shanghai Catalog—
In the cards Justice is blind, carrying scales and a sword.
You will know her when you see her. Hope she's on your
side.

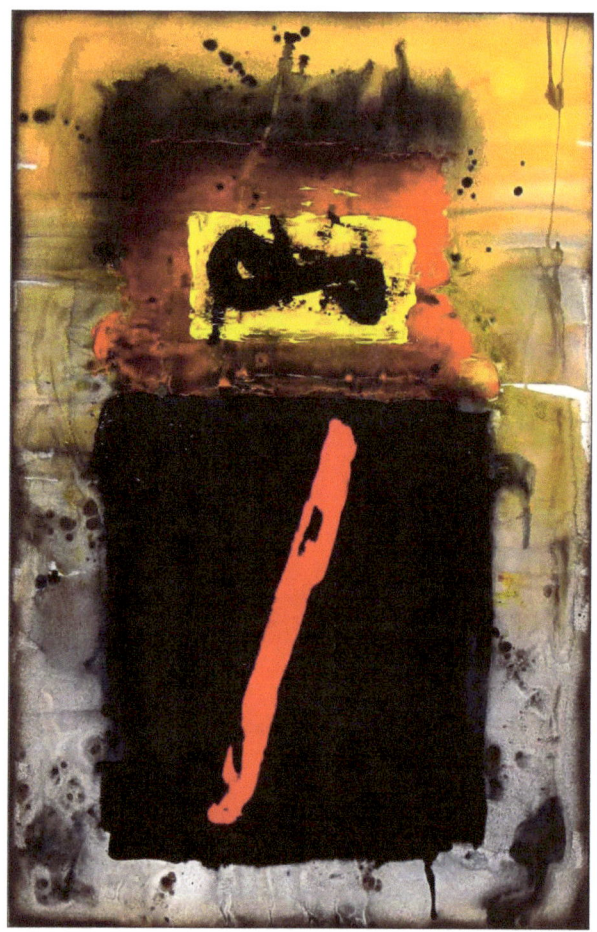

Tarot XI. The Chariot.
(dated 3/7/95)

From the 1995 Shanghai Catalog—
The Chariot is your triumphal car until you are dumped in the dirt like everyone else.

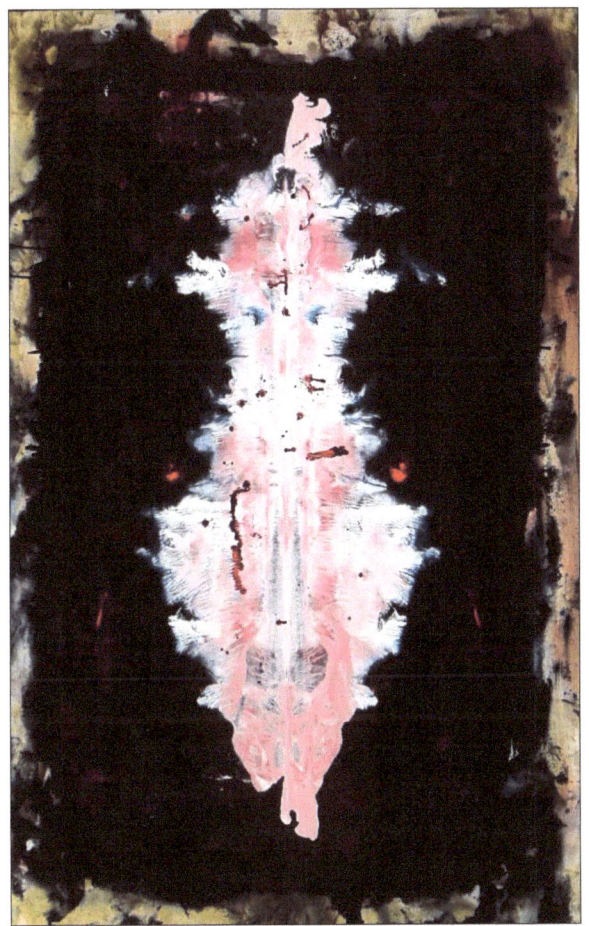

Tarot XV. Devil
(dated 4/8/95)

From the 1995 Shanghai Catalog—
The Devil is the hunger you feed with your desire: the poison that feels so good until it kills you and then it's gone.

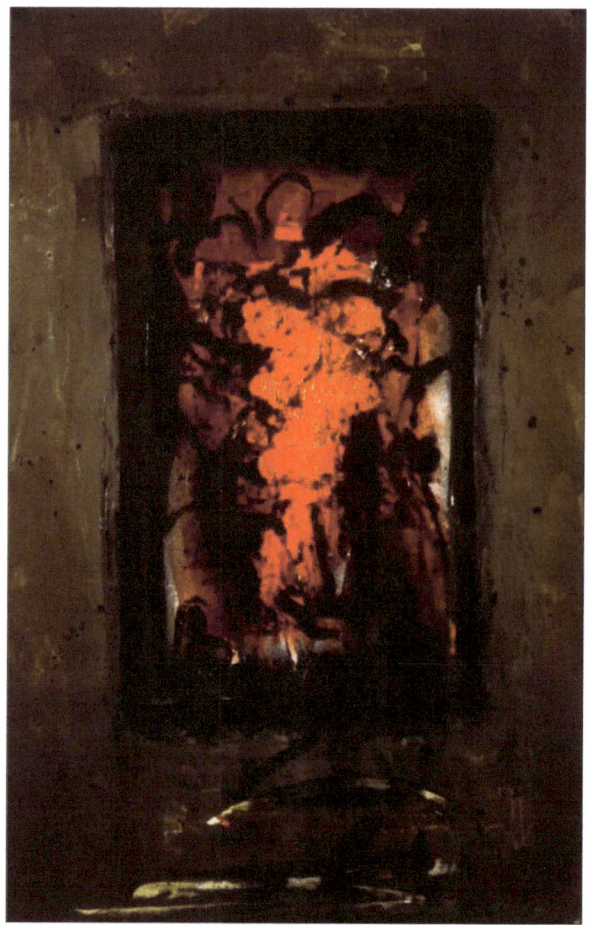

Tarot XV. Devil
(dated 4/9/95)

From the 1995 Shanghai Catalog—
The Devil is the hunger you feed with your desire: the
poison that feels so good until it kills you and then it's
gone.

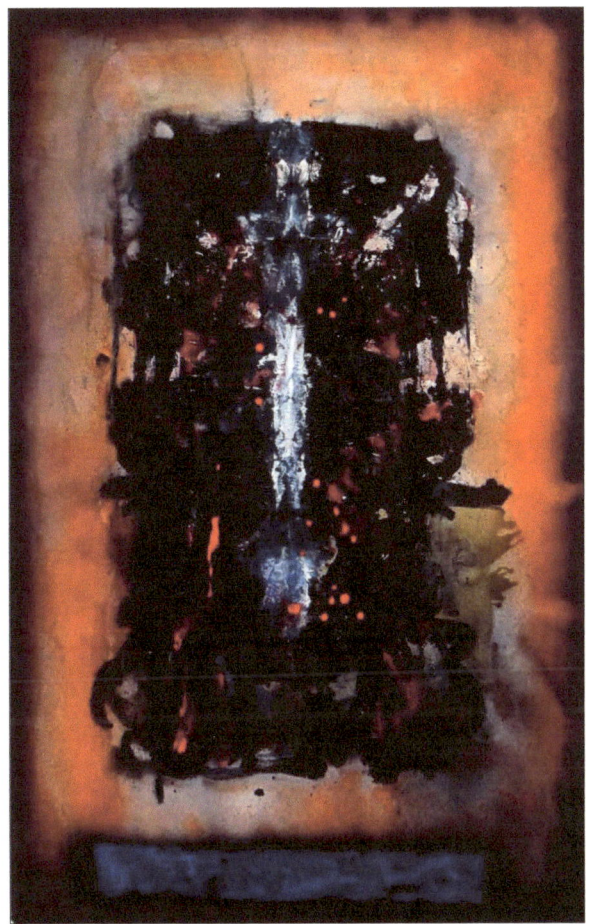

Tarot XV. Devil
(dated 4/11/95)

From the 1995 Shanghai Catalog—
The Devil is the hunger you feed with your desire: the poison that feels so good until it kills you and then it's gone.

19

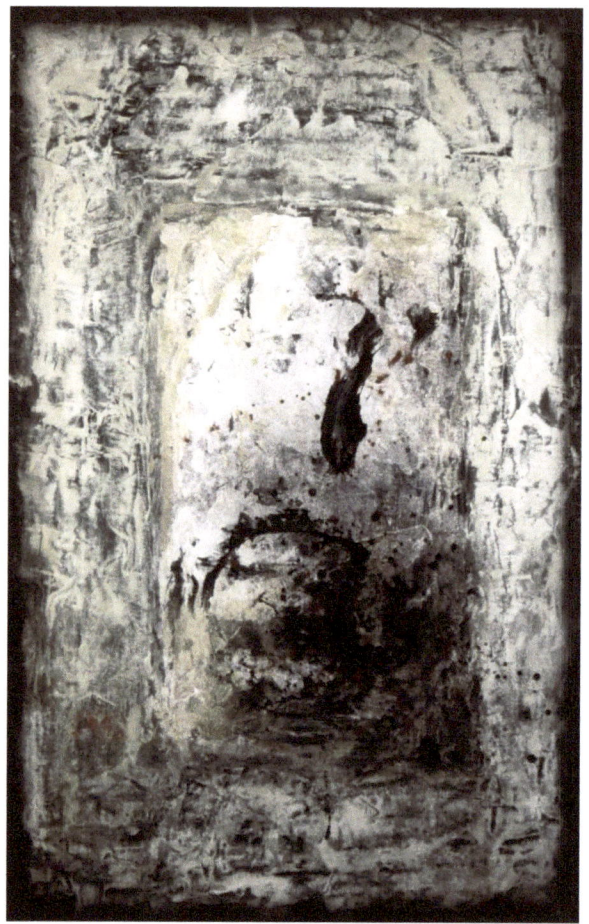

Tarot XVIII. Moon
(dated 6/28/95)

From the 1995 Shanghai Catalog—
The Moon is darkness engulfing you in a shimmer of silver
and gray.

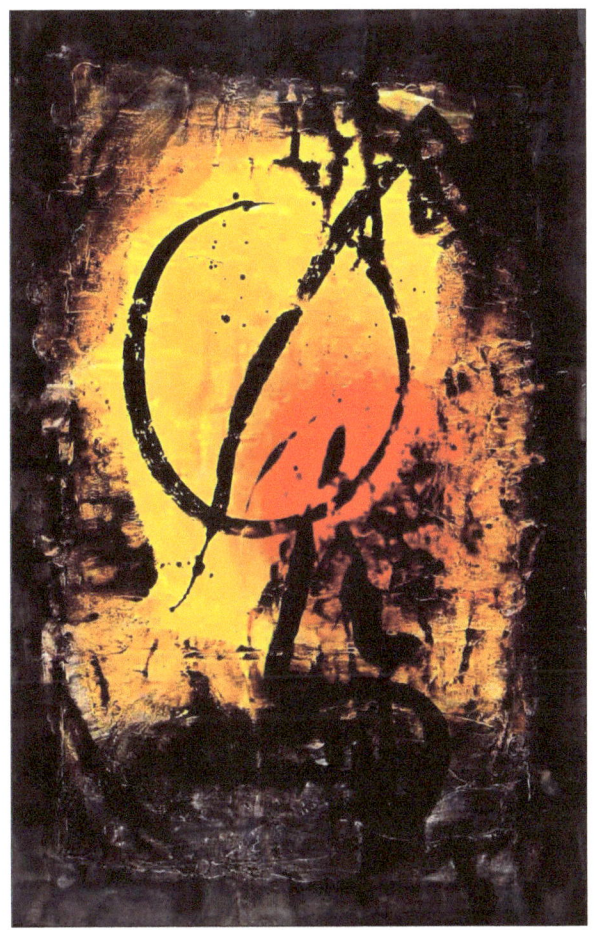

Tarot XIX. Sun
(dated 5/5/95)

From the 1995 Shanghai Catalog—
The Sun is the fire you caught but it escaped.

Tarot from the minor Arcana

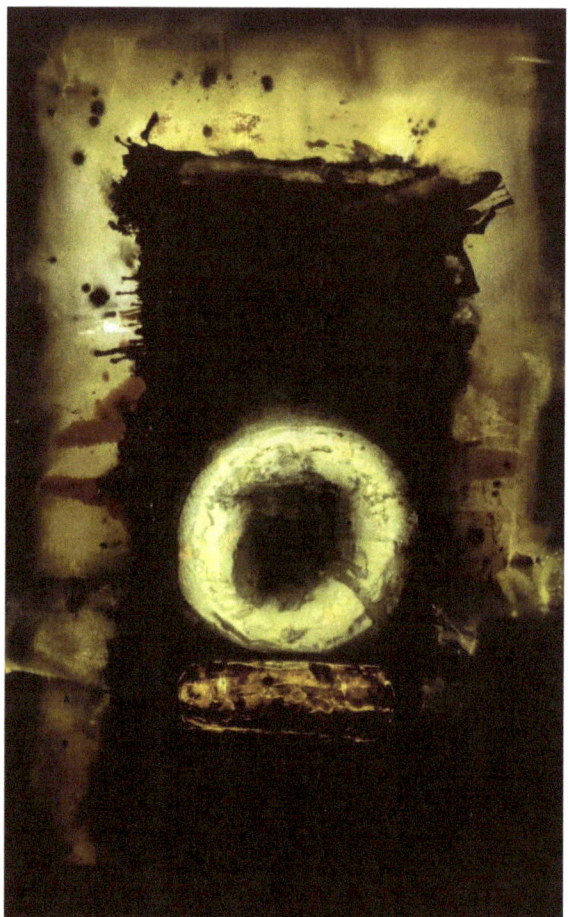

The Ace of Coins
(dated 3/8-9/95)

From the 1995 Shanghai Catalog—
The Coin is the golden mark of market value. Nearly
worthless as metal, it carries every value humans can give
to it.

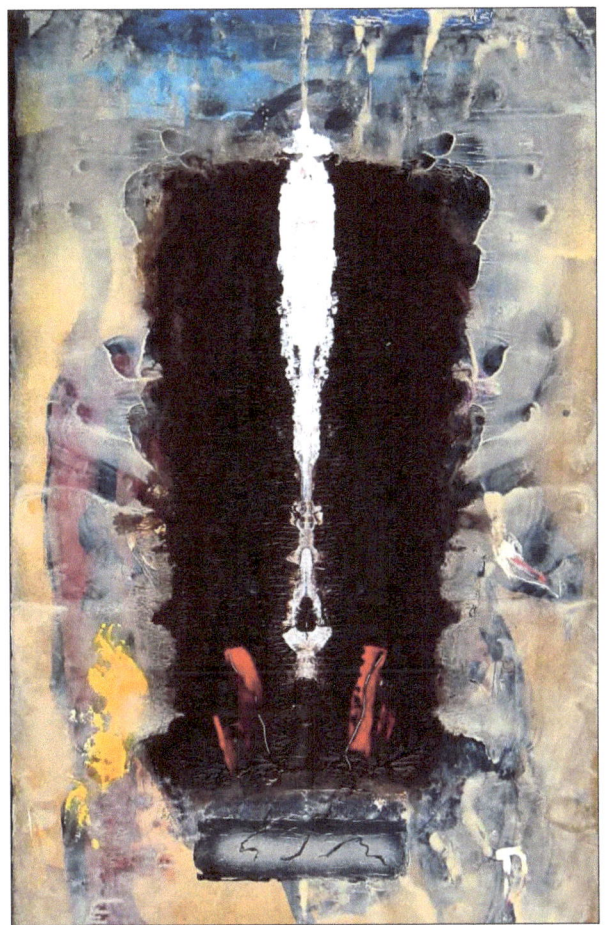

The Ace of Swords
(dated 4/29/95)

From the 1995 Shanghai Catalog—
Both the Coin and the Sword are man-made, are metal and
of the spirit and masculine when compared to the Club and
the Cup[4] which are "natural," of wood or of plants and
growth, of the earth and feminine.

---

[4] Refers to the other two suits of the Minor Arcana. The four suits are
Stave (Club), Cup, Coin and Sword.

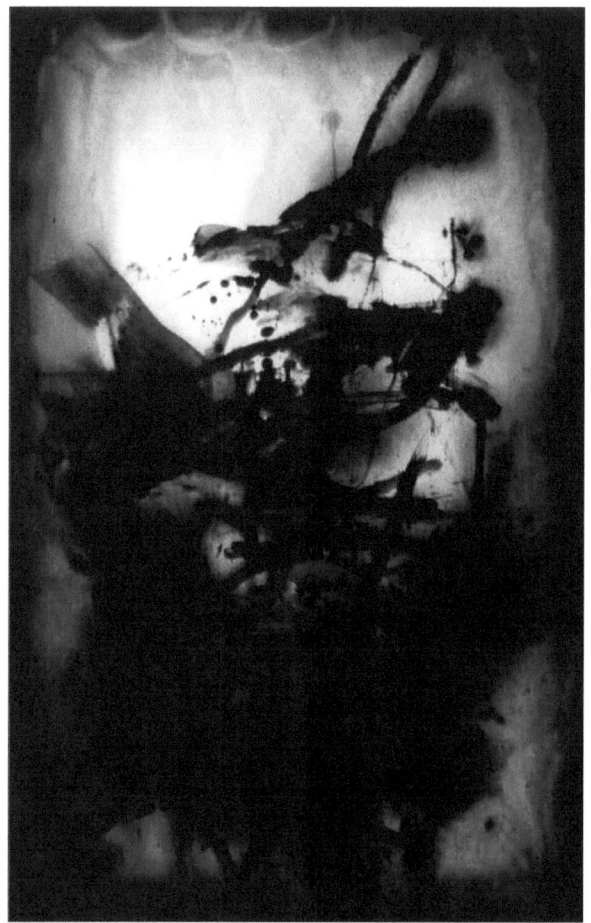

A Knight
(dated 3/12/95)

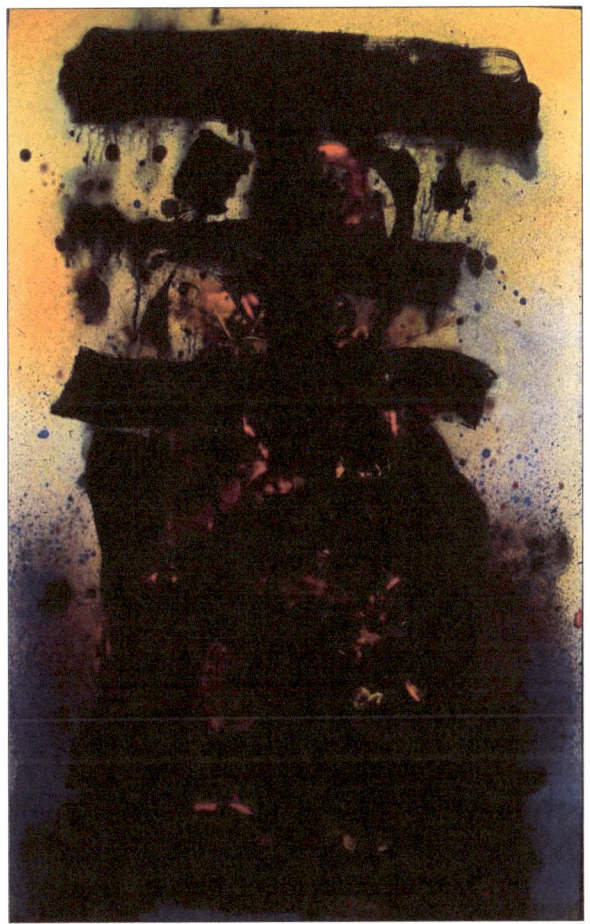

(Undated and unmarked from the 1995 period of the Tarot set.)

Don't ask me for a reference.
See what you see, find your own.

That was 1995. This is 2011. Now what?

The occasion of this exhibition suggested to me that I might explore the Tarot imagery in paint again after now some sixteen years. The question came which cards to pick, and so that I would be deprived of personal choice I used a "numerological" method to convert whatever was the date that day to the number for a Major Arcana card to paint that day.

The next eight pages are the images from January – February 2011 presented in the order of the days of making them.

All of these are acrylic on paper, 40 x 27 inches.

January 7, 2011

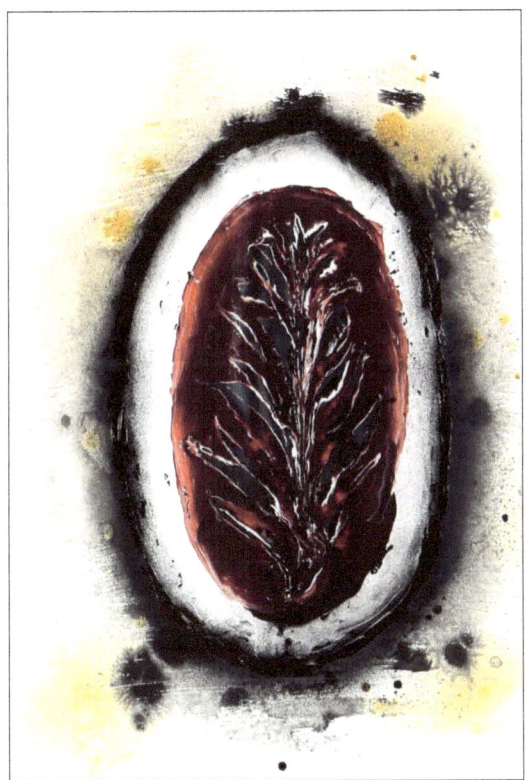

III. Empress.
#2, January 2011.

How she flowers and feeds, ever always onwards 'til she's over.

January 14, 2011

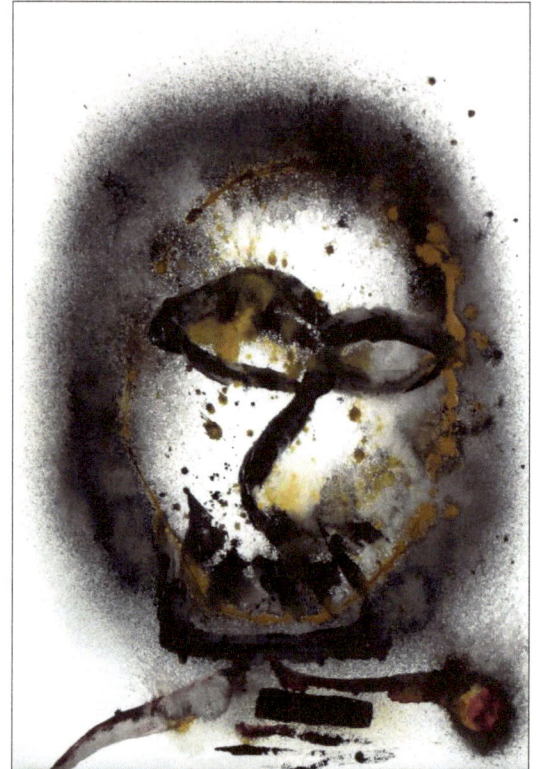

XIII. Death
#4, January 2011.

S'nuff said.

January 15, 2011.

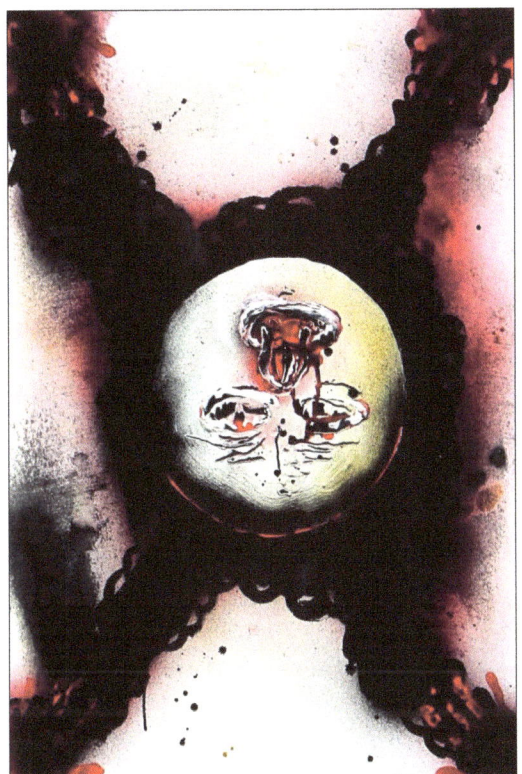

XII. Hanged Man
#5, January 2011.

From the 1995 Shanghai Catalog—
In the cards the Hanged Man hangs tied by one foot upside down—and his clothes fall open to the ashes below calling to the blackness within.

January 22, 2011.

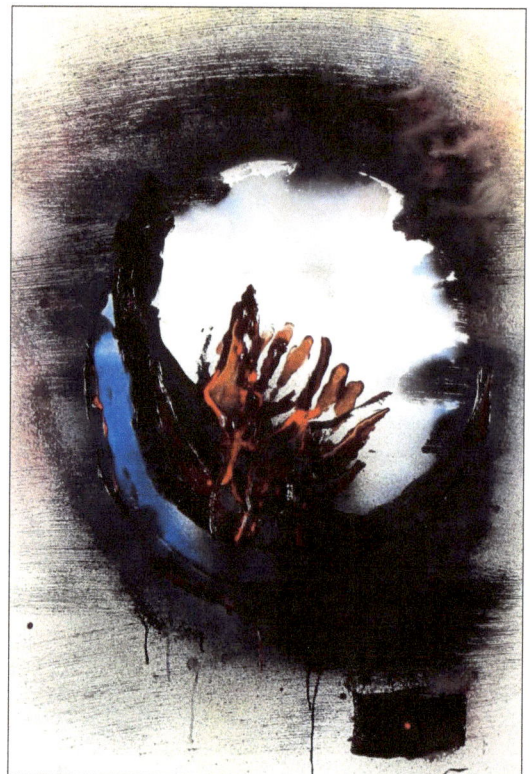

XVIII. Moon.
#6, January 2011.

Though you claw to catch, he always fades away.

January 24, 2011

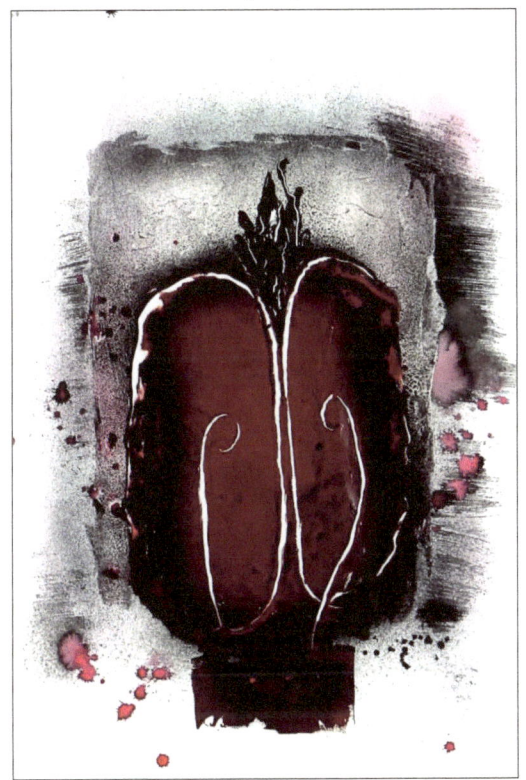

XV. Devil.
#9, January 2011.

For guys, she's the sweet little bitch; for gals, she took
your guy (unless you're her).

January 26, 2011.

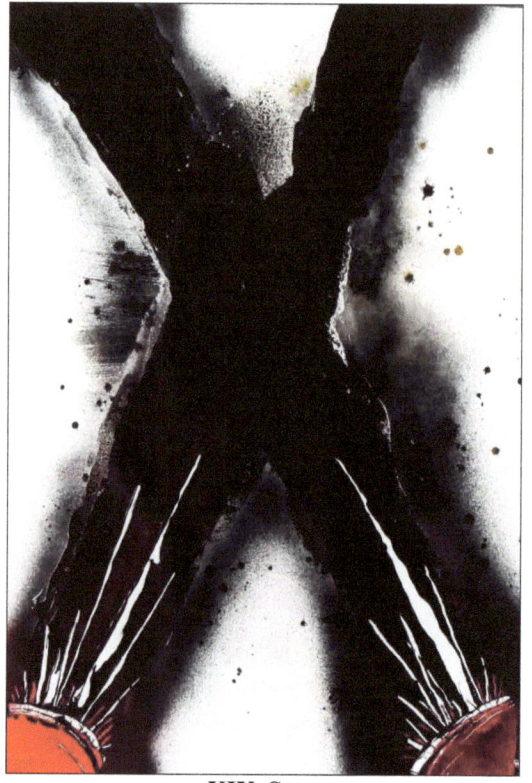

XIX. Sun.
#10, January 2011.

From the studio notes about this painting—
" Sunrise, sunset,
the years go round…
Que sera sera"

February 9, 2011.

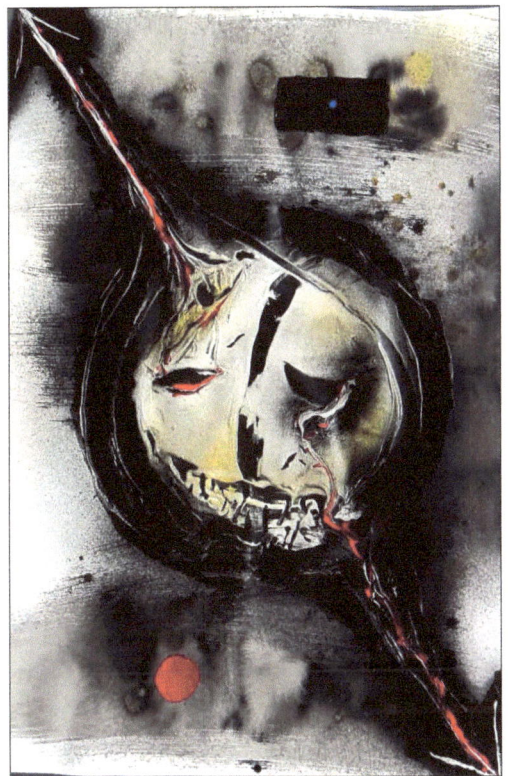

XX. Judgment.
#1, February 2011.

From the studio notes about this painting…
Which way to go, up or down, Hell or Heaven?

February 12, 2011.

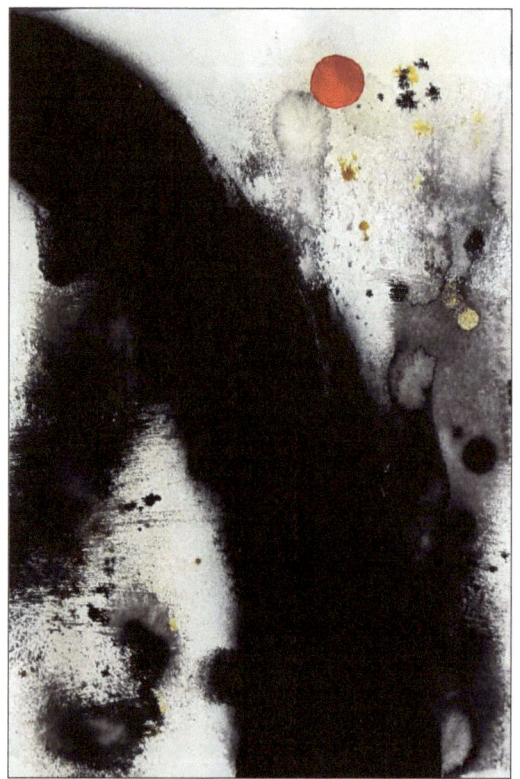

X. Wheel of Fortune.
#2, February 2011.

From the 1995 Shanghai Catalog—
The Wheel of Fortune is the chase for gold, pride, power and glory, a delusion spinning in your face. Time turns, what went up must come down. The sun is forever.

The Tarot works were from the spring of 1995 and from January and February of 2011. Here for variety and to finish it off are a few pieces from 2010.

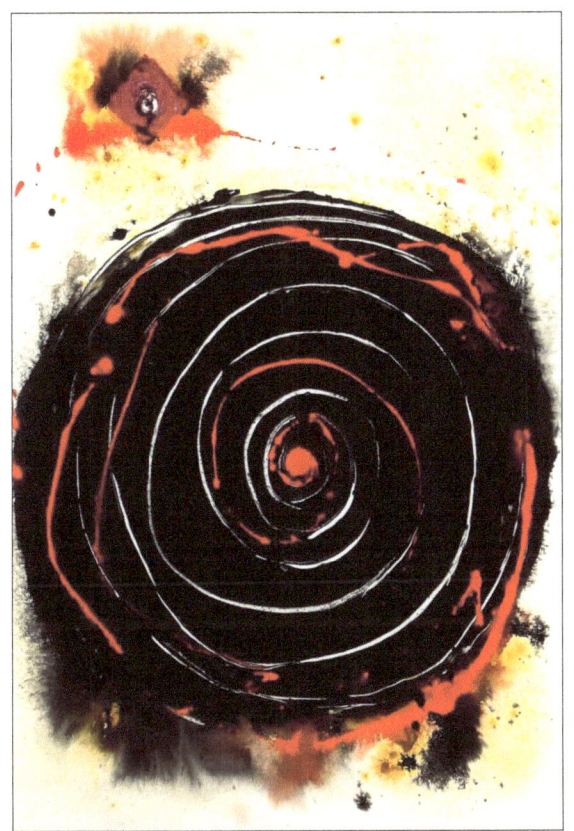

#1 June 2010
Acrylic on paper, 44 x 30 inches.

From my studio notes about this painting:
#1 June is life and death always together
in the spiral of time.

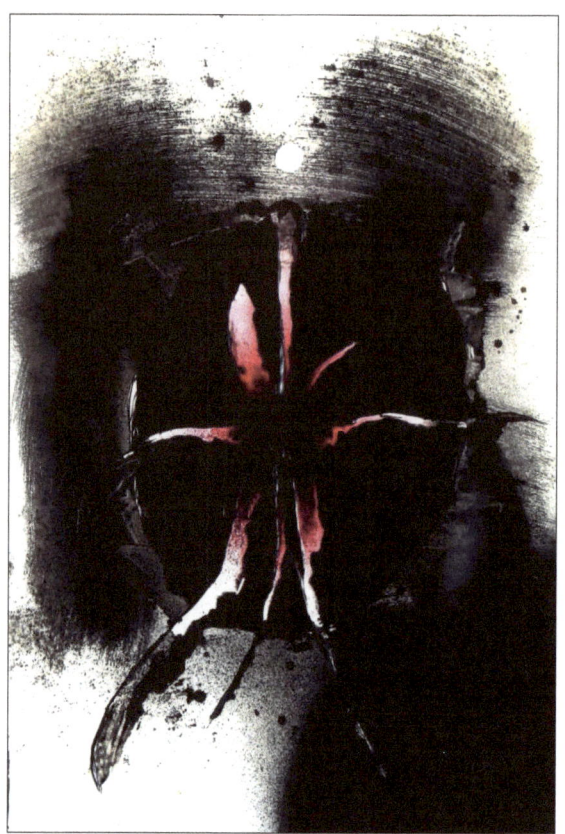

#2 September 2010.
Acrylic on paper, 44 x 30 inches.

From my studio notes about this painting:
"Smoldering, ever smoldering
Caught between earth and sky
on a night of full moon."

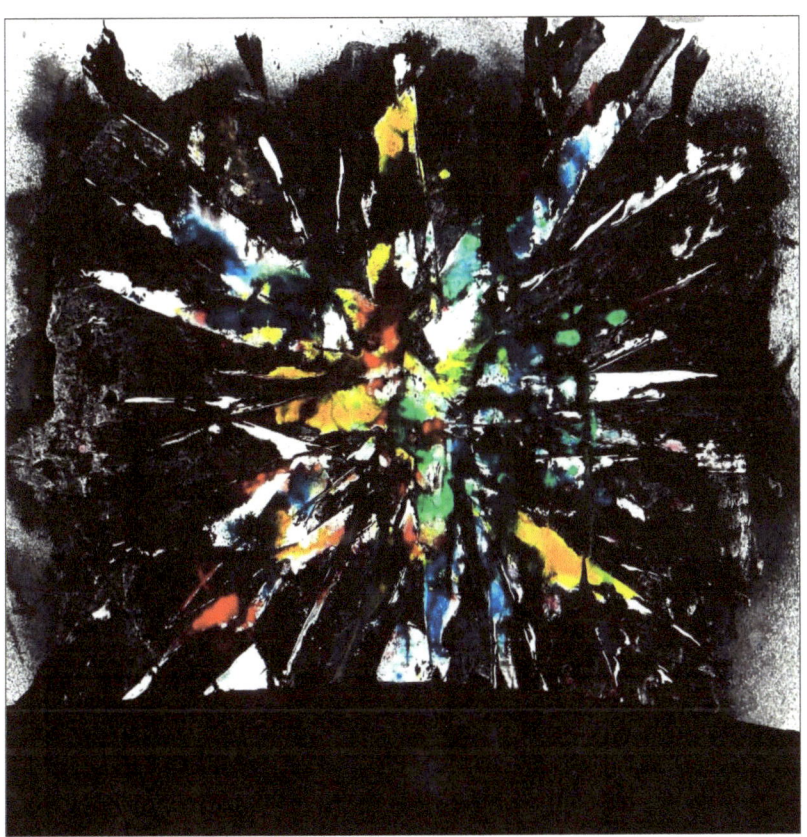

 # 1 November 2010
Acrylic on paper, 44 x 30 inches.

From my studio notes about this painting:
"Looking at this painting in its final form with the dark earth base, I heard 'A fragment of a faith affirmed'."

FRED MARTIN RESUME

Fred Martin was born 1927 in San Francisco. He received the BA (1949) and MA (1954) degrees from the University of California at Berkeley, also studying at the California School of Fine Arts (now the San Francisco Art Institute) under David Park, Mark Rothko and Clyfford Still.

Martin's first solo show was in 1949 at the Contemporary Gallery in Sausalito, California; his first group exhibition was the 1949 Annual Exhibition of Painting and Sculpture at the San Francisco Museum of Modern Art.

Martin's most recent one person exhibitions are

2011	Art Foundry Gallery, Sacramento, California
	Gallery DeNovo, Sun Valley, Idaho
2009	Art Foundry Gallery, Sacramento, California.
2007	Gallery DeNovo, Sun Valley, Idaho
2006	Knorr Gallery, San Mateo, California
2004	Paul Sunderholm Gallery, San Francisco
	Collectors Gallery of the Oakland Museum of California
2003	Retrospective at Oakland Museum of California
	Retrospective at Sanchez Art Center, Pacifica, California
	Ebert Gallery, San Francisco
2001	Ebert Gallery, San Francisco
2000	Ebert Gallery, San Francisco
1999	Ebert Gallery, San Francisco
	Han Art Contemporain, Montreal, Canada
	Ebert Gallery, San Francisco
	Shasta College Gallery, Redding,
1997	Ebert Gallery, San Francisco
	Arts and Consciousness Gallery,
	John F. Kennedy University, Berkeley, California
1996	Frederick Spratt Gallery, San Jose
1995	Shanghai University College of Fine Arts, Shanghai, P.R.C.

Previous solo exhibitions include the M.H. de Young Memorial Museum and the Richmond Art Center as well as a mid-career retrospective at the San Francisco Museum of Modern Art.

Martin's awards include a grant from the NEA and both Bronze and Gold Medals from Annual Exhibitions at the Oakland Museum of California.

Martin's work is in the collections of SFMOMA, the Achenbach Collection of the Fine Arts Museums of San Francisco, the Oakland Museum of California, the Richmond Art Center, the Crocker Art Gallery, the Iris and B. Cantor Center for Visual Arts at Stanford University, the Whitney Museum of American Art, the Museum of Modern Art in New York, and numerous private collections.

Martin's artist's books include *Four Decades*, *Lessons from the Masters*, and *Paintings and Studio Notes, January-December 2008*, (all 2009) Green Gates Press, Oakland, California; *From an Antique Land* (1979 and Second Edition 2009), Green Gates Press, Oakland; *A Travel Book* (1976), Arion Press, San Francisco; and *Beulah Land* (1966), Crown Point Press, San Francisco;

Martin's work in art criticism, history and cultural theory has appeared in The Art Journal, Artforum, and Art International. He was Contributing Editor to Artweek, 1976-92, with over 300 essays under the general title *Art and History*. Martin has given many papers in the fields of art criticism, history and cultural theory. His most recent were *Old Age Style and Late Style*, at the 2007 American Psychological Association Convention in San Francisco, *My Life as an Artist* in 2003 at the Oakland Museum, and *How I Make a Painting* at the 2001 American Psychological Association Convention in San Francisco, *Representation and Critique* at the 1997 American Psychological Convention in Chicago, and *A Great Reversal, American Painting 1950-1965* at the 1997 Symposium on Art and Emotion for the International Association for Empirical Aesthetics in Perm, Russia.

Fred Martin is Dean of Academic Affairs Emeritus and Associate Professor of drawing and painting at the San Francisco Art Institute.